ESFJ: Understanding &
Relating with the Provider
MBTI Personality Types Series

During the journey never
lose sight of who you
are.

Miguel

By: Clayton Geoffreys

Table of Contents

Foreword 1

An Introduction to MBTI 4

The Four Dimensions of the MBTI 7

Why is the Myers-Briggs Type Indicator Significant? 12

Uncovering the "Providers": Who is an ESFJ? 14

Why are ESFJs Indispensable Leaders? 19

The 7 Greatest Strengths of an ESFJ 22

    1.   Graciousness 22

    2.   Warmth and Sensitivity 23

    3.   Great at Building and Maintaining Connections ...24

    4.   Leadership 24

    5.   Organization 25

    6.   Strong Sense of Responsibility 26

    7.   Loyalty 26

The 5 Greatest Areas of Improvement for an ESFJ 28

    1.   Extreme Concern Regarding Social Status 28

    2.   Resistance to Change 29

    3.   Neediness 30

    4.   Extreme Selflessness 31

    5.   Vulnerable to Criticism 32

What Makes an ESFJ Happy?....................................34

What are Some Common Careers of an ESFJ? 37

Common Workplace Behaviors of an ESFJ 42

    ESFJs as Employees...43

    ESFJs as Supervisors...44

    ESFJs as Colleagues..45

ESFJ: Parenting Style and Values...........................47

Why Do ESFJs Make Good Friends? 51

ESFJ Romance 55

    Best Personality Matches for ESFJs..........................58

Weaknesses...58

Strengths...59

7 Actionable Steps for Overcoming Your Weaknesses as an ESFJ 62

    1.   Widen Your Perspective 62

    2.   Don't Take Things Personally 63

    3.   Remember Your Needs Too 64

    4.   Communicate More Efficiently 65

    5.   You Are More than What Others Think of You 65

    6.   Loosen Up 66

    7.   Accept That Nobody Is Perfect 67

The 10 Most Influential ESFJs We Can Learn From 68

    1.   Pope Francis 68

    2.   Desmond Tutu 68

    3.   Larry King 69

    4.   Barbara Walters..70

5.   Sam Walton 70

6.   Harry Truman 71

7.   Andrew Carnegie...72

8.   Hugh Jackman 72

9.   Prince William...73

10. Elton John..74

Conclusion 75

Final Word/About the Author.......................................78

Foreword

Have you ever been curious about why you behave certain ways? Well I know I have always pondered this question. When I first learned about psychology in high school, I immediately was hooked. Learning about the inner workings of the human mind fascinated me. Human beings are some of the most impressive species to ever walk on this earth. Over the years, one thing I've learned from my life experiences is that having a high degree of self-awareness is critical to get to where you want to go in life and to achieve what you want to accomplish. A person who is not self-aware is a person who lives life blindly, accepting what some label as fate. I began intensely studying psychology to better understand myself, and through my journey, I discovered the Myers Brigg Type Indicator (MBTI), a popular personality test that distinguishes between sixteen types of individuals. I hope to cover some of the most prevalent personality

1

types of the MBTI test and share my findings with you through a series of books. Rather than just reading this for the sake of reading it though, I want you to reflect on the information that will be shared with you. Hopefully from reading *ESFJ: Understanding & Relating with the Provider*, I can pass along some of the abundance of information I have learned about ESFJs in general, how they view the world, as well as their greatest strengths and weaknesses. Thank you for purchasing my book. Hope you enjoy and if you do, please do not forget to leave a review! Also, check out my website at claytongeoffreys.com to join my exclusive list where I let you know about my latest books. To thank you for your purchase, you can go to my site to download a free copy of *33 Life Lessons: Success Principles, Career Advice & Habits of Successful People*. In the book, you'll learn from some of the greatest thought leaders of different industries on what it takes to become successful and how to live a great life.

Cheers,

Clayton Geoffrey

An Introduction to MBTI

Personality assessments have been steadily growing more popular. If you have ever killed time surfing the Internet, chances are you have taken a personality quiz or two. Many corporations and organizations have begun to rely on personality evaluations as part of their employee hiring process. A popular example of these assessments is the Myers-Briggs Type Indicator (MBTI) test.

The MBTI test is a questionnaire devised to assess a person's decision-making and perception. It analyzes an individual's personality framework and can be extremely helpful in determining their communication style, preferred work environment, and general interests. The Myers-Briggs test also actuates the similarities and differences between people and enables more harmonious interpersonal relationships.

It was first published in 1962 by psychological

theorists Isabel Briggs-Myers and her mother, Katharine Cook Briggs; the MBTI test is one of the oldest personality tests in existence. The mother-daughter team began developing the test in the 1940s to measure people's cognitive preferences in how they made decisions and viewed the world. They first came up with the idea after a lengthy study of Carl Jung's proposed typological theories. Jung published the book *Psychological Types* in which he theorized that there are four primary functions by which people perceive the world. Myers and Briggs took Jung's theories further by creating the MBTI test. Their original goal was to help women determine which jobs during the war would be the best fit for them. Since then, the MBTI test has grown to become one of the most widely taken personality assessments in the world. In the United States alone, the MBTI test is taken nearly two and a half million times each year.

The Myers-Briggs test asks a vast array of questions

based on the theory that all our choices, even the seemingly erratic ones, are actually consistent and not random at all. At the end of the assessment, each individual is provided with a four-letter acronym. Each letter represents the person's score for each dimension: extroversion (E) vs. introversion (I), thinking (T) vs. feeling (F), sensing (S) vs. intuition (N), and judging (J) vs. perceiving (P).

There are sixteen possible results for the Myers-Briggs test: ISTJ, INFJ, INFP, INTJ, INTP, ESTP, ESTJ, ESFP, ESFJ, ENFP, ISTP, ISFJ, ISFP, ENFJ, ENTP, and ENTJ.

Each of these results is highly insightful and can be extremely beneficial in assessing your own weaknesses and strengths, as well as how to overcome them. Knowing another person's Myers-Briggs personality type will also help you understand their motivations, skills, interests, and how to get along with them.

The Four Dimensions of the MBTI

The Myers–Briggs Type Indicator (MBTI) test theorizes that there are four dimensions or pairs of preferences that make up a person's personality framework. Each dimension represents a basic area of an individual's personality. The four dimensions are extroversion (E) vs. introversion (I), sensing (S) vs. intuition (N), thinking (T) vs. feeling (F), and judging (J) vs. perceiving (P). An individual's personality is assessed using a 16-type system based on how they score in each dichotomy.

First, let's look at extroversion and introversion. In the final results of the MBTI exam, E or I will be the first letter used to generalize one's behavior. There's only one word needed to summarize the two, and that is *energy*. An extrovert gets energy from socializing with other people. They are generally outgoing, like big crowds, more spontaneous and perform better in social situations compared to an introvert. On the other hand, introverts lose energy through prolonged social interactions. They draw their energy from solitude and reflection. Unlike extroverts, they need to think before speaking or acting. Because of this, they can be seen as antisocial and unconfident.

Sensing vs. Intuition describes how someone makes sense of the world around them. Somebody that processes information based off their five senses (hearing, seeing, tasting, touching, smelling) is considered an S. They prefer concrete and tangible realities: looking at the details of a situation only trusting what they can process at the moment, as opposed to the larger picture. Conversely, an intuitive describes the world through an unconscious filtering mechanism that adds meaning, creates metaphors and lets them see possibilities in ordinary things. They value first impressions and gut feelings. They are also abstract thinkers and can read between the lines. A person possesses both sensing and intuition, although one is stronger than the other. To give an example, imagine that you're looking at a book. What do you see? Generally a sensor spends time carefully observing the cover, the inch-wide spine, the name of the author and the styling of the letters. Meanwhile, an intuitive looks at a book and thinks *story*. They aren't as focused on the psychical details of the book; so much as they are the theory of possibilities that unravel once you open it and start reading.

Feeling vs. Thinking is self-explanatory. They are decision-making functions. They indicate the process by which an individual arrives at a certain choice or course of action. If somebody is typed as a feeler they base their decisions in life on personal gut instincts and their own emotional judgment on a subject. They are more subjective. They are believers in the motto "follow your heart." This makes them more empathetic with other people, but it also means that they are more sensitive and tend to get hurt easily. Thinkers can

9

detach themselves from a situation, which allows them to make choices from a critical, purely objective standpoint. They appreciate logical explanations to a phenomenon and want to know the verifiable facts.

Judgment vs. Perception is the function people use when viewing the outside world. It is based on scheduling, organization, and the speed at which one makes their decisions. A person possesses both a judging function and a perceiving function. Although, just like the other functions, one is more prevalent and used more often in one's daily life than the other. A judgment type enjoys having a planned out routine in life. They do their best working within a schedule and meeting deadlines. They can work quickly to get things done. A perceiver takes life by the hour; they don't enjoy making plans so much as going with the flow. They're still able to meet deadlines just as well as a judging type, but can struggle if having to follow a set routine while getting there. They tend to be more relaxed and carefree.

Why is the Myers-Briggs Type Indicator Significant?

The significance of the Myers-Briggs Type Indicator lies in its inherent value when used in practical applications that enable greater self-awareness and a deeper understanding of others. The test also identifies the differences and similarities between people. This knowledge can pave the road toward more harmonious relationships in the workplace, at home, and in other social situations. On a personal level, knowing your MBTI score also aids in the evaluation of your own weaknesses, strengths, and natural inclinations.

Since its inception, the MBTI test has had numerous practical applications. It is widely used in a number of business-oriented situations such as job selection, employee interviews, and career development. The MBTI test also provides individuals with a tool to recognize potential possibilities for personal success.

In this day and age, self-awareness and an understanding of others are valued strengths. Understanding your own MBTI result could be the first step toward self-growth. It could also lead to a better self-acceptance. Besides, learning how other people act and perceive things can be very valuable when it comes to conflict resolution. If you work with a team, the MBTI can help you identify gaps in your team's dynamics and allow you to work together more effectively.

Uncovering the "Providers": Who is an ESFJ?

ESFJ is one of the 16 Myers-Briggs personality types. It is the second most common personality type, comprising roughly 12% of the general population. The acronym stands for Extroverted Sensing Feeling Judging.

In a nutshell, ESFJs are lovers of people and pleasantries. They are naturally driven to care and provide for other people. They are most comfortable wherever a strong foundation of order and structure is present.

The cognitive functions of ESFJs are as follows:

• Extroverted Feeling (Fe) – Extroverted Feeling is an ESFJ's dominant function. It involves a desire to connect with people which is manifested through being polite and other social graces. ESFJs strive to create

14

harmonious relationships and are attuned to other people's needs.

• Introverted Sensing (Si) – Introverted Sensing is an ESFJ's auxiliary function. It involves gathering information using the five senses and comparing the current situation to similar ones from the past. ESFJs draw from previous experiences to form realistic expectations about what will happen in the future. Because ESFJs are sensors, it takes them a while to see the bigger picture. They will see the trees before noticing the forest.

• Extroverted Intuition (Ne) – Extroverted Intuition, ESFJ's tertiary function, relates to the interpretation of hidden meanings. It involves the coming together of multiple thoughts and ideas to explore a number of alternatives.

• Introverted Thinking (Te) – Introverted Thinking involves the need for rational explanations

15

for actions and conclusions. This process is most commonly utilized when gaps in logic are noticed.

ESFJs are also known as Providers. The Provider is one of the 16 role variants closely associated with the Myers-Briggs Type Indicator.

As Providers, ESFJs are extremely invested in other people's welfare. By nature, they are caring, warm-hearted and sensitive. Their sensitivity is more developed than other types. They have an innate understanding of other people's emotions. In fact, ESFJs can always be counted on in times of sadness, triumph, and celebration. They are always willing to provide their time, energy, and resources to ensure that their loved ones' needs are met.

ESFJs enjoy social interactions. Their core characteristics make them excellent hosts or hostesses. They are great at taking charge during social events such as reunions, parties, and other endeavors that entail people skills and organizing. At a gathering, look for the people who are constantly making sure that no one is left out or in need of anything. They are most likely ESFJs.

ESFJs love people. They enjoy making and maintaining friendships. They are outgoing, confident, and exceptionally friendly. As social butterflies, they have no qualms about starting a conversation with a stranger. In fact, they will happily carry a conversation with anyone about any given topic. They always remember birthdays and anniversaries, and they love celebrating milestones with family and friends. Their social network is constantly fluctuating and expanding.

ESFJs have a strong sense of how people should relate to each other, and they often seek out responsibilities that will allow them to enforce that sense of order. In the workplace, ESFJs possess a knack for maintaining a sense of camaraderie within a team, thus making them excellent leaders. They value authority and

17

adherence to rules, and they work in a structured and timely manner. On a larger scale, ESFJs find comfort in obeying the law and observing customary ceremonies. Even though they might not fully understand the reason behind them, following pre-existing guidelines can make ESFJs extremely happy.

Why are ESFJs Indispensable Leaders?

The four preferences of ESFJs make them indispensable leaders. Their extroversion makes them confident and lively. Their sensing enables them to remain practical and realistic. Their preference for feeling provides them with warmth and compassion. Their judging gives them order and dedication. All in all, they strive toward harmony and rapport while enforcing structure and organization.

ESFJs are sensitive, polite, and productive. These words also perfectly describe their leadership style. From managing conflict between feuding coworkers to being in charge of hosting company events and gatherings, ESFJs will go above and beyond to ensure that everything is running smoothly.

As leaders, ESFJs are able to maintain the balance between keeping their employees happy and making sure that all the necessary tasks are accomplished in an efficient and timely manner. Because they are people pleasers with excellent organizational skills, they are great at motivating their team toward a specific goal. They enjoy working with other people, and they continuously strive to create a supportive environment for all members of their team.

Tradition is something ESFJs value tremendously. Therefore, they respect adherence to rules and organizational hierarchy. In turn, they expect their employees to do the same.

ESFJ leaders are generous with praise and personal attention. They make it a point to let people know when a job is performed well. Furthermore, they know how to make their employees feel valued and appreciated. On the other hand, ESFJ leaders are very critical. They have a strong sense of loyalty and commitment, and they expect others to possess the same inclinations. Therefore, the judging aspect of their personality makes them impatient when their employees aren't performing as expected.

The 7 Greatest Strengths of an ESFJ

Extroverted Sensing Feeling Judging (ESFJ) types have a number of admirable qualities. If you are an ESFJ, you have plenty of strengths that are unique to your personality type. By recognizing these strengths, you can nurture them even more, facilitating personal development and potential success. Here are a few of your greatest strengths:

1. Graciousness

Graciousness is one of the core characteristics of an ESFJ. ESFJs are predisposed to strive toward harmony, rapport and peaceful living. They believe that there is an appropriate way to behave in any given situation. They are always courteous, polite, and well mannered. They are highly conscious about how they deal with other people and will go through great lengths to avoid any form of conflict. They will always look for a win-win solution whenever a problem

22

arises; hence, making ESFJs highly cooperative team players. They are also invaluable in situations that require conflict resolution.

2. Warmth and Sensitivity

Warmth and sensitivity are traits that are regularly associated with ESFJs. Due to their preference for Sensing, ESFJs are known for being warm hearted and sympathetic toward the feelings of other people. They are naturally in tune to the needs of others and are always eager to give their time and resources to ensure the welfare and well-being of those around them. In fact, a big part of their own personal satisfaction comes from the happiness of other people. ESFJs love being able to help and provide, especially in practical and tangible ways that reap immediate benefits for others. However, this can work against them if someone starts to take advantage of their generosity.

3. Great at Building and Maintaining Connections

ESFJs are great at building and maintaining interpersonal connections. This is one of their greatest strengths. They are very outgoing and friendly. They possess a strong desire to feel like they belong and are most comfortable when surrounded by a crowd. As extroverts, they love connecting with people. It's no surprise that making new friends comes so easily to them, and conversations are never boring. They can spend hours catching up with old friends and are always genuinely interested in what's happening in the lives of their loved ones. They are never ones to forget a birthday or anniversary. ESFJs are great listeners. They love learning about the specific details of someone's life, and when they listen, they remember.

4. Leadership

ESFJs possess strong leadership qualities. They also

24

possess an innate need to enforce order. Therefore, it comes naturally for them to oversee events and spearhead tasks. Not only are they action-oriented and responsible, they are also able to create a fun and comfortable working environment for all members of their team. They praise generously and know how to make their employees feel valued. ESFJs are excellent role models and motivators. As leaders, they hold their employees to the same standards they hold for themselves, while staying focused on supporting their team.

5. Organization

Organization is another admirable strength of an ESFJ. ESFJs value structure and order. They love planning ahead and become extremely happy when their plans are followed through. Other personality types might find rituals and routines boring, but not ESFJs. ESFJs consider routines and guidelines very important. They know exactly what needs to be done and they know exactly how to do it. It's highly unlikely for an ESFJ to change their course of action midway through. Having a plan makes ESFJs feel more in control of their lives and environment.

6. Strong Sense of Responsibility

ESFJs are very responsible and dependable. They are extremely dedicated to their duties. They will never leave a task unfinished, especially if they've committed to it. They are loyal to their responsibilities and will often forego their own personal needs just to fulfill their commitments and obligations. When paired with their desire to help and provide, their sense of responsibility enables them to assist others in fulfilling their obligations as well.

7. Loyalty

ESFJs are extremely loyal. They tend to put their partner's needs before their own because of their caring and nurturing nature. They will not hesitate to sacrifice their own happiness for that of other people. In addition, stability is very important as they find comfort in things familiar and secure. Because of this, they will try their best not to disrupt the status quo. This quality makes them extremely loyal to their partners. Similarly, their loyalty extends to friendships and the workplace. However, that same loyalty makes it hard for them to accept a difficult truth about a loved one or friend.

The 5 Greatest Areas of Improvement for an ESFJ

ESFJs possess many strong, positive qualities. Conversely, there are also areas in which an ESFJ's personality may require improvement. Note that these qualities should not be viewed as limitations, but as opportunities for growth. Awareness is the first step toward self-improvement and personal development.

1. Extreme Concern Regarding Social Status

A notable area for improvement is ESFJs extreme concern in regards to their social status. Not only do ESFJs want to be liked, they also view themselves as a reflection of the society in which they live. They thrive on social interactions and being part of a crowd. They value what other people think about them. In fact, a big part of their personal satisfaction stems from knowing that they are socially accepted. While this enables them to build connections and expand their social network, it also leads to excessive worrying about their status. Because they are preoccupied with how they are perceived by society, ESFJs have a tendency to limit themselves. They shy away from thoughts or actions that might come across as too extreme or different, which might end up stunting their open-mindedness and imagination. Sometimes, they will go so far as to sacrifice their own opinions entirely just to agree with the majority. Their incessant worrying about how others see them can also lead to ESFJs becoming insecure and developing low self-esteem.

2. Resistance to Change

ESFJs are driven by Extroverted Feeling, which relates to the perception of ideas, situations and life in general. This makes ESFJs uncomfortable with unfamiliar territories. They possess a "place for everything and everything in its place" perception of the world. When ESFJs feel as though their view of the world is challenged, they instinctively shut out the new information. They value rituals and routines, and can be very resistant to change. They think, "It worked before, there's no reason it shouldn't work again." They may snap or react harshly to any disruption to their established schedule. They also find it very hard to step out of their comfort zones. Their discomfort with things that are new to them can also be related to their need for social approval. They view their status quo as the norm, and transitioning to something that is new to them elicits fear of acceptance or appearing too unconventional. Another factor that contributes to ESFJs' discomfort with change is their strict adherence to rules and guidelines. When they encounter an idea or situation that differs from what they know to be right, ESFJs will stick to what they are accustomed to.

3. Neediness

ESFJs can be needy. They require approval and positive affirmation from other people to be happy.

They want to be valued and appreciated, and they want it shown and expressed. It is extremely common for ESFJs to fish for compliments, especially when they feel that they are being undervalued or ignored. Their perpetual need for positive feedback can be tiresome and annoying, especially for people with a different personality. When an ESFJ feels neglected, it weighs heavily on them, more so than any other personality type. Even when the neglect is only imagined (an unanswered phone call or a missed appointment), ESFJs dwell on the perceived rejection for a long period of time.

4. Extreme Selflessness

ESFJs are providers. They love being able to help other people and are naturally attuned to other people's needs. However, their selflessness and generosity can also become liabilities. ESFJs tend to put their own needs last. Be it in the workplace or in personal relationships, ESFJs put the happiness of others before

31

their own and can be self-sacrificing to a fault. As a result, they will go out of their way to make sure that the people around them are happy and provided for, often neglecting their own well-being. They might also choose to help someone else with a task or project and postpone their own.

5. Vulnerable to Criticism

ESFJs are very sensitive by nature. When you add their need for approval factor you get someone who can be very vulnerable when presented with real or perceived criticism. ESFJs are extremely gracious and will go out of their way to avoid conflict, so any form of criticism regarding their habits or beliefs will hurt them deeply. When criticized, ESFJs will feel cornered, causing them to act defensively. They are even more vulnerable when the criticism comes from someone whose opinion they deeply respect. When they find themselves in situations of conflict such as this, they have a hard time seeing the facts and tend to feel attacked. Moreover, an ESFJ's definition of conflict differs from other people. What another person may view as harmless banter or a lively discussion, an ESFJ might perceive as the beginning of a potential argument.

What Makes an ESFJ Happy?

ESFJs are called Providers for a reason. Caring and providing are core aspects that make them who they are. They love being able to lend a helping hand and are always willing and happy to do so.

ESFJs are among the most social of the personality types. As extroverted feelers, they come alive when they find themselves in the company of others. It could be small talk with a new acquaintance, long conversations with a few old friends, or a party with fifty people, ESFJs find joy in such interactions. Their network is constantly in flux. The only thing that makes ESFJs happier than social interplay is being certain that they are well liked and appreciated. An ESFJ's happiness is inextricably tied to how they are perceived by others; therefore, ESFJs are happiest when they feel valued and accepted by those around them.

ESFJs go through great lengths to maintain the relationships they have built with others. They enjoy doing things to take care of their friends and loved ones. A sure way to return the favor is to show them that their efforts are valued and reciprocated. A phone call to let them know they are remembered, an invitation to go out and catch up, and small displays of affection are a few ways to make an ESFJ happy. Try not to make them feel neglected or disregarded.

During conversations, ESFJs prefer talking about the lives of their friends and colleagues. They love offering advice about personal problems or sharing joy in moments of triumph. Topics like these are certain to pique an ESFJ's interest. However, conversations that lean toward the abstract, such as science or philosophy, do not interest ESFJs.

In other facets of their lives, including the workplace, ESFJs are happiest when a strong foundation of structure and order is present. As mentioned, they find comfort in the familiar. To keep an ESFJ happy, avoid disrupting the smooth flow of their routine. Organization is key and nothing irks an ESFJ more than when their plans are changed midway or when established rituals are not observed. For those ESFJs that are in positions of authority, respect is crucial. When their authority is questioned or challenged, ESFJs will take it personally.

What are Some Common Careers of an ESFJ?

Esfjs enjoy working in areas that give them the power to be in charge over other people. They like to wrap their hands around the needs of a situation, and give people certain tasks accordingly. None of these jobs are set in stone-anyone can be great at whatever it is they want to do; although an ESFJ might feel most comfortable with these jobs that highlight their functions, and their temperament.

• Education - Pursuing a career in education requires strong interpersonal and organizational skills. You have to be able to relate to other people while maintaining a formal and structured atmosphere. These are qualities that ESFJs possess in spades. In fact, surveys have found that ESFJs are the most represented personality type among Education majors, and 80% of elementary school teachers are ESFJs.

37

ESFJs are extremely comfortable assuming authoritative roles, especially if the position enables them to interact and mingle with other people. They are also naturally skilled at putting others at ease. When combined with their warm and sensitive nature, these qualities makes ESFJs perfectly suited for teaching jobs. Elementary school seems to be the most popular choice among ESFJs pursuing education. This is probably because elementary school aged children are more eager to learn and are easier to please.

• Nursing - Nursing is another career where ESFJs excel. By nature, ESFJs are excellent caregivers. They enjoy helping people, especially in practical ways. Nursing, as a profession, provides ESFJs with an avenue to exercise their inclination toward caring for others. Their dependable and organized nature is also aligned to the characteristics of a career in nursing. ESFJs possess keen attention to detail and are very observant. These qualities are valued assets in the world of nursing and enable ESFJs to pick up on important signs about their patient's health. At the same time, their ability to remain focused on the task at hand ensures that their mind does not stray while performing procedures or dealing with patients. Working as a nurse requires a high level of organizational skills. There are routines to follow and rules to adhere to. This aspect of nursing will appeal to any ESFJ. Nurses are also highly appreciated in the workplace, and ESFJs find positive affirmation highly rewarding. Not only will ESFJs make great nurses, they are also likely to gain immense personal satisfaction from this career path.

• Counseling/Social Work - ESFJs possess an uncanny ability to make people feel immediately at ease. They know exactly which questions to ask to get someone to open up. Even though you have just met them, ESFJs never feel like strangers. This quality is a very valued strength when pursuing a career in counseling or social work. Not only does social work allow ESFJs to provide assistance to people in need, but because it is a job that requires face-to-face interactions, it also appeals to their extroverted nature. Social work also provides ESFJs with a traditional and structured working environment.

• Physical Therapy - Another career path suited for ESFJs is physical therapy. Physical therapy requires a great deal of empathy. Patience and dedication are also required. For other personality types, helping and caring for people with disabilities could prove to be tiring and extremely challenging, but ESFJs thrive in such situations. They find great personal satisfaction in being able to motivate people toward recovery. This career path will also appeal to an ESFJ's desire to be positively perceived, because the job allows them to affect and change people's lives for the better.

• Church Worker/Volunteer - ESFJs are generally

40

active in their respective communities. They also possess genuine concern about the welfare and safety of those around them. They will not hesitate to provide their energy and time to help and support other people. These are all qualities that make ESFJs excel as church workers or volunteers. This job allows ESFJs to immerse themselves in a helping role that supports a large number of people.

Common Workplace Behaviors of an ESFJ

In their professional lives, ESFJs are friendly and outgoing (extroverted). They pay close attention to details (sensing). They generously praise their colleagues (feeling) and firmly adhere to the organization's rules and guidelines (judging).

An ESFJ's overall workplace demeanor can be described as enthusiastic and action-oriented. They like to take on projects that will directly involve them with other people, and they prefer tasks that have real, practical benefits. If you ask someone to describe their ESFJ colleagues, you might hear the words responsible, helpful, and dedicated.

During moments of conflict in the workplace, ESFJs will attempt to say or do something to neutralize the situation. Whenever possible, they will try their best to look for a win-win solution. However, because they

42

are so uncomfortable with conflict, they might agree to a temporary remedy that will ease the situation for the meantime. ESFJs are highly sensitive and interpret things at face value, so they tend to misread heated discussions and regular office banter as indications of conflict.

Since they are judgers, ESFJs flourish in working environments where there are clear and specific guidelines to be followed. They rely on schedules and procedures. They need to know exactly what is expected of them and how their performance is being assessed. When a sense of order is not present in the workplace, an ESFJ will try to create it whenever possible.

ESFJs as Employees

As employees or subordinates, ESFJs are focused, determined, and responsible. They are very efficient workers, especially when presented with straightforward and clearly defined tasks. They value structure and are very respectful toward their managers and supervisors. They do not mind completing monotonous tasks. In fact, routine work is something ESFJs find comfortable. They have no problems with punctuality and meeting deadlines. They are hardworking individuals, making them well liked and respected in the workplace. When a task is assigned to them, ESFJs are very focused. They will not abandon a task or project and will see it through until it is complete. It is almost impossible for them to leave a project hanging, even when completing it is no longer required. They also dislike moving forward with a task if there is no clear plan in place. They work best with a specific goal to work toward.

ESFJs as Supervisors

ESFJ supervisors or managers are well liked and popular in the workplace. They make it a point to remember the names of all their employees. They work hard to ensure that everyone is getting along and that each member of the team feels involved. They are appreciative of other people's input and ideas. If a task is performed well, ESFJ leaders are generous with praise and positive affirmations. However, if a job is not completed according to their standards, they can become impatient. They also react negatively when their authority is challenged. ESFJs are somewhat set in their ways. When new suggestions are brought to the table, an ESFJ supervisor might have a difficult time considering them, especially if the suggestions are unconventional.

ESFJs as Colleagues

ESFJs love making new friends wherever they go. The same goes for the workplace. They will take their time to get to know their colleagues and are very approachable. They are excellent team players. They are highly cooperative and are always involved. They believe that working together and getting along is just as important as reaching their goal. Their caring nature is also highlighted in the workplace. They are always the first to lend a hand or support a struggling teammate. They are also quick to motivate colleagues who seem to need inspiring. However, ESFJs are extremely sensitive and vulnerable to criticism and rejection. If their offer to help is rejected, ESFJs might take it personally.

ESFJ: Parenting Style and Values

As people, ESFJs are gracious, pleasant, and polite. These qualities are also evident in their demeanor as parents. They believe in behaving appropriately in any given situation, and they want their children to do the same. Respect and obedience is crucial.

Children raised by ESFJs may describe their parents as both strict and caring. ESFJs have a firm notion of how one should and should not behave. They also exercise a "work before play" mentality. However, the innate caring nature of an ESFJ is amplified when it comes to their children. They have no trouble showing affection. Even when it comes to discipline, ESFJs are able to establish their authority without coming off as cold and uncaring.

ESFJ parents are hugely concerned with their children's safety and well-being. This is notably evident in new parents caring for babies. Infants are

47

highly dependent and rely on their parents for everything, and ESFJs relish being able to support them and provide for their needs. As their children begin to mature, they start to care about them even more. Sometimes, ESFJ parents can be perceived as over protective and controlling. They desire to keep their children out of harm's way and tend to take charge over the majority of their children's lives. They decide who their children play with, which clothes they should wear, and what activities they can become part of. Although their intentions are good, ESFJs parents should let their children explore and make mistakes that will lead to social and emotional development. If not, their children may end up going through a rebellious phase.

It's perfectly normal for growing children to pull away and distance themselves from their parents, especially when they enter puberty. However, ESFJs are very sensitive and may get their feelings hurt when their kids become teenagers. As their children begin to grow distant, ESFJ parents may attempt to delay their independence and keep them reliant.

ESFJs value respect and authority, and they expect their children to obey and respect them as well. They do not react well when they are disrespected or when their rules are not followed. Still, ESFJs are feelers and can empathize with other people's feelings, so they may find it very hard to punish their kids when they misbehave. This leads most ESFJ parents to turn to more subtle (but arguably less effective) methods of disciplining their children, such as using guilt to manipulate them into better behavior. This is an area ESFJ parents need to work on. If they are unable to discipline their children effectively, their kids might grow up with a murky concept of right and wrong.

Children of ESFJs are always well taken care of. Their needs, especially the physical ones, are always fulfilled. They are also likely to grow up in an organized environment where boundaries and rules are clearly established.

When adults raised by ESFJs were asked about their upbringing, most of them fondly recalled being cared for and showered with affection. They described their parents as warm and loving. However, they also mentioned that their parents could sometimes be nitpicky and controlling. Even as adults, some complained about their ESFJ parents not giving them enough space and constantly offering unsolicited advice.

In a nutshell, ESFJs are affectionate and caring parents who make sure that their children are raised in a structured environment where their needs are met. They are constantly concerned with their children's welfare and want what is best for them. However, they can sometimes be perceived as strict and controlling.

Why Do ESFJs Make Good Friends?

Anyone who has ever had an ESFJ friend can attest to their genuine warmth and kindness. They are nice, friendly, and approachable. They naturally gravitate toward people, and people are drawn to them as well.

While other extroverted personality types have a large number of acquaintances and a small group of friends, ESFJs will have multiple groups of close friends that they value equally. Their social network is constantly growing. Not only do they make friends easily, but they are also tireless in making sure that the bonds they create remain strong.

ESFJs have no trouble making friends. They are outgoing and confident, and they will not hesitate to walk up to someone, introduce themselves, and begin a conversation. They are comfortable around strangers, and make them feel comfortable around them too. Unlike other personality types, ESFJs enjoy small talk.

They possess a natural ability to make a person feel at ease. ESFJs love getting to know people, and they instinctively know the exact questions that will get a person to open up to them. They enjoy conversations about other people's lives and are genuinely fascinated by the stories people share.

While ESFJs are great at meeting new friends, they are even better at maintaining friendships and connections. ESFJs are very popular, and they often have a large set of friends in multiple circles. Their nurturing personality shines through in the way they support and care about their friends. They are willing to do whatever they can to make their friends happy. They never turn down a friend in need. However, as much as they enjoy being able to help and provide, ESFJs expect to be valued and appreciated in return. It can be very hurtful if ESFJs feel as though their efforts aren't being reciprocated.

They are keen, detail-oriented observers. They notice

the small things. An ESFJ friend will be able to tell if you're having a bad day or if you're excited about something. Their ability to read the tiny details enables them to foresee the needs of their friends. They know if you need a shoulder to cry on. They can tell if you want someone to talk to. ESFJ friends can see these things and can make their friends feel special and cared for.

ESFJs are very protective of their friends. They are the type that will always have your back. In any argument, they will always take your side. However, their loyalty can sometimes turn into a liability. Because they think so highly of the people they care about, ESFJs can be blind to the flaws of their friends. When confronted with an ugly truth about one of their friends, an ESFJ will turn a blind eye or be unable to see their friend's negative qualities.

ESFJs are organized extroverts. They love putting together and overseeing social events and gatherings such as parties and reunions. They also make excellent hosts. Their homes are most likely welcoming and designed for entertaining.

ESFJ Romance

ESFJs are social creatures who value relationships above all else. They are deeply committed and service-oriented. Their happiness is dependent on the happiness of their partners. As lovers, they are affectionate, supportive, and loyal. If you are an ESFJ, read on. You may find some useful insight unique to your personality.

ESFJs are traditional and place high importance on customs and rituals. In the context of relationships, ESFJs are respectful of established norms. They will dutifully go through all the stages of a relationship: courtship, dating, and so on. Unlike other personalities, EFSJs find little joy in casual encounters and random flings. Meaningless hook-ups do not thrill them. They seek out serious and long term relationships that are mutually fulfilling. Even during the early stages of a romantic relationship, an EFSJ will already be thinking about the future and the possibility of marriage and raising a family. They want stability and will do their best to fulfill their roles. They are very conventional and are fond of observing long established dating practices. A male ESFJ will show up at his date's house with a bouquet of flowers and a reservation to a fancy restaurant, while a female ESFJ will want her date to do those things for her.

ESFJs delight in celebrating relationship milestones. They never forget a birthday or anniversary. Furthermore, they enjoy organizing gatherings and parties, so every occasion gives them a chance to indulge their love for company and celebration. Sound familiar?

Because they are providers, ESFJs will do whatever it takes to give their partners everything they need, both physically and emotionally. They are selfless lovers who will always put the needs of their mate before their own. This quality can sometimes work against them. ESFJs tendency to sacrifice their own well-being may eventually cause their partner to take them for granted. In worst case scenarios, their relationship might turn emotionally abusive.

As people, ESFJs abide by a strict moral code. You live lives of structure and order, and they expect their mates to do the same. You need clear and concise guidelines. In a relationship, an ESFJ might attempt to create rules that make the relationship run more smoothly. Furthermore, ESFJs possess an innate desire to take charge and enforce boundaries. Although their intentions are good, their actions might be seen as controlling, especially if their partner has a more carefree and flexible personality.

ESFJ lovers can sometimes be perceived as manipulative, especially in situations of conflict. They dislike confrontations and arguments make them feel uncomfortable, thus, they resort to more subtle methods when they feel wronged. Instead of confronting their partners, ESFJs prefer a more passive approach such as the silent treatment or making their significant others feel guilty.

Best Personality Matches for ESFJs

People of any personality type can be in a fulfilling relationship, but certain types have natural tendencies that happen to mesh well together. The most ideal partner for an ESFJ is someone with an ISFP or INFP personality. Introverts are not as expressive as extroverts, and being in a relationship can be mutually beneficial for the both of them. In addition, someone with an inclination toward perceiving can help ESFJs learn how to loosen up and be more open minded. If you are an ESFJ, you will find some (if not all) of these qualities familiar.

Weaknesses

• They require acknowledgment and appreciation. They need to know that they are valued. If they feel neglected, they can become needy and demanding.

- They need structure. Boundaries and rules are important to them. This can come across as controlling and smothering to other personality types.

- They are vulnerable to criticism and uncomfortable with conflict. They resort to avoidance or guilt manipulation to avoid confrontation.

- They are self-sacrificing to a fault and value the happiness of their partner more than their own. In some cases, they will neglect their own health and well-being just to provide for the people they care about.

- They can be blind to the flaws and shortcomings of their partners. If they find out something bad about the person they love, they will choose not to believe it.

Strengths

- ESFJs will exhaust their time and resources just to ensure that their partners are happy and cared for. They will put the needs of their loved ones before their

59

own.

- They are organized, responsible, and service oriented. They can be relied on to take charge of everyday necessities.

- They are extremely loyal and committed. They seek out long term and mutually fulfilling relationships.

- When it comes to intimacy, they are a great sexual partner. They are naturally affectionate and eager to please.

- They are a keen observer who pays attention to details. They notice the little things and are attuned to the moods and emotions of their partners.

- Because of the judging aspect of their personality, they are good at budgeting and other money-related matters.

- They are outgoing, energetic, and fun to be

around.

7 Actionable Steps for Overcoming Your Weaknesses as an ESFJ

There is no fool-proof formula for success. People, regardless of their personality type, have different dreams, plans, and goals that are uniquely their own. However, individuals with the same personality type possess similar inclinations and innate tendencies that have certain strengths and weaknesses. The first step toward personal growth is awareness of one's areas for growth.

If you are an ESFJ, here are some actionable steps to overcome your weaknesses. Remember. Your weaknesses are not limitations. They are opportunities to expand your strengths.

1. Widen Your Perspective

As an ESFJ, you are set in your ways. You adhere to a strict moral code that might be hindering you from seeing the bigger picture. Things that are new and foreign can be scary, and the idea of embracing something that goes against everything you know can be even scarier. However, you have to recognize that ideas that are different from yours are not as threatening as you think. They can often be doorways to a wider understanding of how the world works. Start embracing new possibilities by taking a moment to remind yourself that the opinions and beliefs of other people, no matter how unconventional, are also valid and worth considering. The world is constantly changing, and there are so many new things to learn.

2. Don't Take Things Personally

If you are an ESFJ, you have most likely felt neglected or undervalued at some point in your life. Understand that not everyone thinks and behaves the same way you do. You are a warm and caring person, and the people around you know this. They certainly appreciate you for the way you inspire and support them. There are times when they might not acknowledge or reciprocate your efforts the way you want them to, but that doesn't mean they don't value your friendship. Take a moment to put yourself in their shoes. They might just be expressing their gratitude differently. They might just be busy. Don't view their actions as personal attacks against you.

3. Remember Your Needs Too

As an ESFJ, you are hardwired to care and provide. That's just who you are. A huge part of your personal satisfaction comes from making the people you love happy. You want to make sure that they are safe, taken care of, and provided for. However, you tend to forget that you have needs too. Don't get so wrapped up in taking care of everyone else that you start neglecting your own health and safety. Every now and then, conduct a self-check. Ask yourself if your needs are also being met. If they are not, take a break and focus on yourself for a while. Relax. Unwind. Pamper yourself. Do something that makes YOU happy.

4. Communicate More Efficiently

You are a peace-loving ESFJ. As much as possible, you try to avoid confrontation. Be that as it may, avoidance only works for so long. If you do not communicate with people in times of stress, they will not know how to identify and deal with the problem at hand. Using guilt to manipulate them is not a healthy solution either. Granted, things might get better for the time being, but if the issue is not properly addressed, it will keep on resurfacing. Rip off the Band-Aid and have that dreaded conversation. As long as you keep a level head and an open mind, it will not be as bad as you think.

5. You Are More than What Others Think of You

You are a social creature. You love making friends and being around people. The happiness of the people you care about is important to you, and you will do everything in your power to make your loved ones feel special. Since you exert so much effort into keeping your friendships strong, you expect to be appreciated and valued. You want your actions to be acknowledged. Being liked is something you strive for. Still, you can't always please everybody. That's just how things are. Sooner or later you will meet someone who will not see you as their cup of tea. That's okay! You are more than what other people think of you. You are not any less valuable as a person just because you do not get along with someone.

6. Loosen Up

Your need for order and structure can sometimes urge you to exert control over your surroundings. Knowing exactly what to expect makes you feel safe, and you may feel uncomfortable in unpredictable situations. In spite of that, you cannot control everything. Some things are just out of your hands. Loosen up a little and try to go with the flow. Pleasant surprises can happen when you least expect it.

7. Accept That Nobody Is Perfect

You are loyal to your friends and loved ones. You always have their backs. You might even say that you would fight to the death for them. Be that as it may, understand that the people you love are fallible human beings. Nobody is perfect. Everyone has made mistakes at some point in their lives. Your loyalty may sometimes blind you to the flaws and faults of your friends and family. Accept that they also have some less desirable qualities and love them anyway.

The 10 Most Influential ESFJs We Can Learn From

ESFJs are well known for being selfless, nurturing, and approachable. When they apply their natural tendencies toward motivating and helping other people, they can accomplish wonderful things. Here are a few inspiring ESFJs that have used their skills and abilities for the betterment of society.

1. Pope Francis

Pope Francis is the current pope of the Catholic Church. Not only has he overseen and taken part in a large number of charitable events, he is arguably one of the humblest and most compassionate popes the world has seen. Even non-Catholics are drawn to his down-to-earth demeanor. People describe his leadership style as warm and approachable.

2. Desmond Tutu

Desmond Tutu is an anti-apartheid activist who fought

for social justice in South Africa. During the apartheid, Tutu organized bloodless marches in Cape Town and used his position as bishop to campaign for harmony among all parties involved. Since the fall of the apartheid, he has remained active in the quest for justice. He has been involved in the fight against HIV/AIDS, poverty, homophobia, and racism. True to his ESFJ nature, Tutu has been quoted as saying, "God's dream is that you and I and all of us will realize that we are family, that we are made for togetherness, for goodness, and for compassion."

3. Larry King

Larry King is an American television host mostly known for his show on CNN, *Larry King Live*. King's most notable qualities as an ESFJ are his great conversational skills and extroverted nature. Like most ESFJs, he possesses the ability to make people feel at ease around him. In fact, he is such an outstanding conversationalist that his interviews do not feel like interviews, but rather two friends catching up. Furthermore, his daughter describes him as traditional, which is another ESFJ trait. King is an excellent example of an ESFJ who developed his natural tendencies to their full potential.

4. Barbara Walters

Barbara Walters is an American journalist and television host. Her outgoing and gregarious personality (a trademark of ESFJs) has greatly contributed to her success. She has hosted several television shows, such as *The View*, *Today*, and *ABC Evening News*. According to Walters herself, part of her success as a TV personality is her ability to incorporate compassion and understanding when conducting interviews.

5. Sam Walton

Sam Walton was an American entrepreneur. He is best known as the founder of the multinational corporation,

Walmart. As a leader, Walton was well liked by his employees. The people he worked with described him as down-to-earth and caring. One of his former employees mentioned that Walton seemed to take a genuine interest in all of the people he worked with. Walton seems to possess all the qualities that make ESFJs indispensable leaders. Like any ESFJ, Walton valued teamwork and sought to create a harmonious working environment for his employees. In an interview, he said, "One person seeking glory doesn't accomplish much; at Wal-Mart, everything we've done has been the result of people pulling together to meet one common goal - teamwork."

6. Harry Truman

Harry Truman was the 33rd president of the United States of America. As an ESFJ, Truman was helpful, considerate, and approachable. He once said that he liked to do things for other people and thought of their troubles instead of his own. His selfless and caring

71

nature is the core characteristics of an ESFJ.

7. Andrew Carnegie

Andrew Carnegie was a self-made industrialist who took charge of the American steel industry expansion. He was one of the wealthiest men during the 19th century. Carnegie was a philanthropist. In fact, he gave away almost 90% of his wealth to multiple charitable institutions. He also wrote an article entitled "*The Gospel of Wealth*" that implored the wealthy to use their fortunes to help improve the society. The article became a catalyst, and it inspired a surge in philanthropy. Carnegie's story is extremely inspiring and heartwarming. He is an excellent example of a selfless ESFJ who puts the needs of other people before his own.

8. Hugh Jackman

Hugh Jackman is an Australian actor who has made a big name for himself in Hollywood. He has starred in a

72

large number of blockbuster films and has garnered international praise and recognition for his roles. As a person, Jackman has been described as genuine, warm, and approachable. True to his ESFJ nature, he enjoys team sports such as cricket, rugby, and basketball. He also possesses the selflessness and generosity of ESFJs. He is a philanthropist who actively lobbies for numerous charitable organizations. He is also a longtime advocate of Microcredit, which provides loans to entrepreneurs who wish to start businesses in impoverished nations.

9. Prince William

Prince William, Duke of Cambridge, is the son of Prince Charles of Wales and the late Princess Diana. At an early age, Prince William was exposed to the struggles of the less fortunate. His mother, Princess Diana, took him and his brother to various centers that housed people suffering from HIV/AIDS. His ESFJ nature led him to continue his charitable contributions.

73

Prince William is also part of an organization that aims to conserve the African wildlife. At the time of his wedding to Catherine Middleton, he implored people to donate their money to charitable institutions instead of giving them wedding presents. The foundation they set up to receive the funds has helped 26 charities to date.

10. Elton John

Elton John is another influential ESFJ. He is an English singer and songwriter, and has sold over 250 million copies of his records worldwide. He has been actively supporting AIDS foundations since the deaths of two of his friends, Freddie Mercury and Ryan White. In 1992, Elton John started an AIDS foundation with the goal of funding programs for HIV/AIDS prevention and eliminating the discrimination that HIV/AIDS-infected people experienced.

Conclusion

In a nutshell, Extroverted Sensing Feeling Judging (ESFJ) types are selfless and dependable providers who thrive in structured environments. They are arguably the friendliest and most outgoing among the personality types. Friends and loved ones of ESFJs can attest to their generous and caring nature. Furthermore, an ESFJ will go through great lengths and will do everything in their power to ensure that the needs of the people around them are fulfilled. They are highly organized and responsible, and they adhere to strict moral codes.

In the workplace, ESFJs are reliable and focused. They value rules and guidelines, and feel comfortable with familiar tasks. When it comes to relationships, they are generous, warm, and affectionate. They seek long term commitments and stability.

However, some of their best qualities can sometimes

turn into liabilities. Their generosity might be taken advantage of, their need for order might be perceived as smothering and controlling, and their desire for constant positive affirmation might lead to self-esteem issues and insecurities. When it comes to managing their expectations of other people and putting things into perspective, ESFJs have to work on furthering their natural strengths and turning their weaknesses into opportunities of self-improvement.

If you are an ESFJ, the descriptions and ideas mentioned in this book may have resonated with you. You probably feel both comforted and unnerved by the fact that a lot of people share your tendencies and inclinations. It can be argued that everyone is unique, regardless of personality type, but understanding the reasons behind your actions and emotions can be highly insightful. You may have learned a lot about yourself from what you have read so far, and self-awareness is first step toward greatness. You may also have picked up a few helpful tips on tapping into your full potential.

In spite of the information above, the Myers-Briggs Type Indicator is not a how-to book. It is not the ultimate answer to your career, relationship, or personal problems. The MBTI is a road map. It shows you how to get to wherever you want to go. The ultimate destination is still your choice and the reins are yours to hold.

Final Word/About the Author

I was born and raised in Norwalk, Connecticut. Growing up, I could often be found spending afternoons reading in the local public library about management techniques and leadership styles, along with overall outlooks towards life. It was from spending those afternoons reading about how others have led productive lives that I was inspired to start studying patterns of human behavior and self-improvement. Usually I write works around sports to learn more about influential athletes in the hopes that from my writing, you the reader can walk away inspired to put in an equal if not greater amount of hard work and perseverance to pursue your goals. However, I began writing about psychology topics such as the Myers Brigg Type Indicator so that I could help others better understand why they act and think the way they do and how to build on their strengths while also identifying their weaknesses. If you enjoyed

ESFJ: Understanding & Relating with the Provider please leave a review! Also, you can read more of my works on *ESTJs, How to be Witty, How to be Likeable, How to be Creative, Bargain Shopping, Productivity Hacks, Morning Meditation, Becoming a Father,* and *33 Life Lessons: Success Principles, Career Advice & Habits of Successful People* in the Kindle Store.

Like what you read?

If you love books on life, basketball, or productivity, check out my website at claytongeoffreys.com to join my exclusive list where I let you know about my latest books. Aside from being the first to hear about my latest releases, you can also download a free copy of *33 Life Lessons: Success Principles, Career Advice & Habits of Successful People.* See you there!

Made in the USA
San Bernardino, CA
05 February 2018